Here's what <u>REAL</u> Buckeyes have to say...

 "After reading "101 Ways to Tell If You're a <u>REAL</u> Buckeye! I realized, I know ALL these people!"—Jim Karsatos, Ohio State Football

 "The ultimate book for people who 'bleed' scarlet and gray!"—Katie Smith, Ohio State Women's Basketball

 "A delightful, humorous book that Buckeye fans are sure to enjoy." —Terry Smith, "Voice of the Buckeyes"

 "A must-read for true ~~blue~~ scarlet and gray fans!"—Ron Stokes, Ohio State Basketball

 "If I weren't already a Buckeye nut, this book would make me one!"—Brutus Buckeye, Ohio State Mascot

To all my Family and Friends...your support, inspiration, and trust made this possible. Thanks Janet, Kathy, Paul, and Kristen for your creativity and talent. To Lorissa, Ann, Jack, Rosa, Jay, and Terri — your help and encouragement has meant a lot.

Many thanks to The Ohio State University Office of Trademark and Licensing Services; The Ohio State University Department of Athletics; The Ohio State University Alumni Association, Inc.; CAPA; WBNS and WOSU Radio; and all the great and enthusiastic Buckeye fans out there.

Special thanks and love to Dave, my best friend and husband extraordinaire, and my terrific Mom!

"Give credit where it's due."

—General George Patton

Book and cover design: Susan Stanton
Illustrations: Paul Isaacs, Kristen March, Janet McGuire, and Kathy Sandrock. Graphic Advisor: Lorissa Dorn

Library of Congress Catalog Card Number: 97-73480
ISBN: 0-9658849-4-5

10 9 8 7 6 5 4 3 2 1

Printed in the United States of America

"101 Ways to Tell If You're a REAL Buckeye!" is available at quantity discounts with bulk purchase for business, sales promotion use, or education. For information, write to Special Sales, Brus & Sasscer, 3000B East Main Street, #354, Columbus, OH 43209.

101 Ways to Tell If You're a <u>REAL</u> Buckeye!

by

Susan Stanton

(alias "Ima Buckeye")

B&S
Brus & Sasscer Publishing

# A Buckeye's Tale...

As I grew up in Iowa listening to all the stories about those crazy Ohio State fans, I never believed I would one day wind up living in Buckeye-ville myself. I had only been in Columbus a few weeks when I began to have second thoughts about moving. I remember telling my mother that I thought there might be some kind of weird disease here. Everyone seemed to be dressed in the same colors—scarlet and gray. Even the houses were decked out in the school colors.

But I did wind up staying and worked at WBNS Radio ("The Voice of the Buckeyes") and WOSU Radio. I even had the chance to meet some of Ohio State's greatest players and experience first-hand the "fan"-atical fans of Ohio State. So it was bound to happen...

I was at my first Michigan game. The Buckeyes had just won the Big Ten Conference and were going to the Rose Bowl. Jets were flying overhead, 92,000 fans were making a thunderous noise, and I suddenly found myself jumping, screaming, cheering, and basically going "nuts." I had it...Buckeye fever! Now all I can say is:

"Let's Go Bucks!"

You know you're a <u>REAL</u> Buckeye when...

1. You carry so many lucky Buckeye nuts in your pockets that you're attacked by the university squirrels on the way to the game.

2. Your wife can't get you to open a can of beans the rest of the year, but on football Saturdays you become the Julia Child of tailgate dining.

You know you're a **REAL** Buckeye when...

You know you're a __REAL__ Buckeye when...

3. All your children's names are "Brutus," even the girls!

4. You go to your high school reunion and brag about the fact that you sat next to someone on a plane, who knows someone, who's related to someone else, who once met the Coach at the grocery store.

5. You get into a fight over who is "The Best Damn Band in the Land."

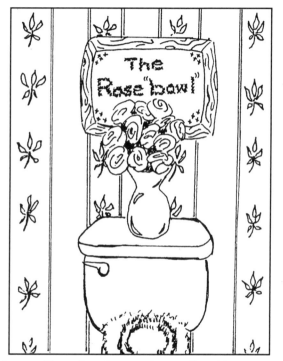

6. You will only clean the toilet if your wife refers to it as the Rose "bowl."

7. The calendar over your bed counts down the days to the start of the next Buckeye football season.

You know you're a __REAL__ Buckeye when...

8. You believe that guy who pretends to be Woody really <u>is</u> Woody.

9. You'd choose dotting the "**i**" in "Script Ohio" over winning a Pulitzer Prize.

10. Your idea of great literature is the Ohio State football and basketball media guides.

You know you're a __REAL__ Buckeye when...

11. You secretly sing "Hang on Snoopy" whenever the band plays "Hang on Sloopy."

12. You start a petition to name the Horseshoe the Eighth Wonder of the World.

13. You believe that St. John Arena was named after the patron saint of basketball.

You know you're a __REAL__ Buckeye when...

14. You give up eating corn because you heard that it is also called "maize."

15. Your third wife stated in the divorce proceedings that you were having an affair with "some nut."

16. You talk about going to the V.C. so much, everyone thinks that's your name.

*You know you're a **REAL**
Buckeye when...*

17. Your wife continually asks you to stop referring to the Thanksgiving turkey as "Wolverine meat."

18. You have the Ohio State Ticket Office on your speed dialer at home and work.

You know you're a **REAL** Buckeye when...

You know you're a __REAL__ Buckeye when...

19. You list your necklace of Buckeye nuts on your home insurance policy under fine jewelry.

20. You don't mess around with those washable Buckeye tattoos—you have a permanent one on your cheek. No, the other cheek.

21. Your bridesmaids' dresses are scarlet and gray.

22. The airport has repeatedly asked you to dismantle your outdoor shrine to Woody. The candles keep confusing pilots.

You know you're a __REAL__ Buckeye when...

23. You hire Martha Stewart as a consultant to improve your tailgate parties.

24. If the Marching Band had a new CD called: *The Ohio State Marching Band Salutes The Grateful Dead*, you'd buy it.

25. When you were about to give birth to your son at the University's hospital, you demanded a room facing the Horseshoe.

You know you're a <u>REAL</u> Buckeye when...

26. In the divorce proceedings, you give up the house, the car, and the boat and keep the season tickets.

27. You hang around the Horseshoe weekday afternoons just to hear the Ohio State Marching Band practice.

28. You've lost three girlfriends this football season alone because you refuse to change your lucky Buckeye underwear.

You know you're a **<u>REAL</u>** Buckeye when...

29. You pretend you are the "Neutron Man" in the shower when they play "Neutron Dance" on the radio.

30. You need two semi-trucks to deliver your supply of chocolate and peanut butter whenever you make Buckeye candy.

You know you're a <u>REAL</u> Buckeye when...

You know you're a __REAL__ Buckeye when...

31. There is so much scarlet in your closet, it starts to bleed through the walls.

32. You had to put an addition on to your house, so you could expand your rec room to look like the stadium.

33. You criticize the other team's band uniforms during the half-time show.

34. You wish the OSU Archery team could play "William Tell" with the Big Ten referees.

You know you're a __REAL__ Buckeye when...

35. You can name and give the stats for every Ohio State Varsity sport, including Synchronized Swimming.

36. You make your own band uniform just so you can get a better seat for the game.

37. The judge warns you again about accosting people on the street just because they happen to be wearing Michigan colors.

You know you're a <u>REAL</u> Buckeye when...

38. You've made a pilgrimage to Woody's old office in the R.O.T.C. building more than 12 times in the past year.

39. You think about starting your own cable station, WBCK..."All Buckeyes All the Time!"

40. You can name every sports bar in town that carries the Buckeye games, including how many TVs they have, their screen sizes, and their menus. All the waitresses even greet you by name.

41. Your convertible has a sticker that reads,
    "This is my <u>other</u> Buckeye tailgate RV!"

You know you're a __REAL__ Buckeye when...

42. You are as giddy as a school girl when you hear about a sale on Buckeye merchandise.

43. The Horseshoe maintenance crew has asked you time and time again not to pull up the field's sod for your own lawn.

44. The Highway Patrol requires you to weigh-in with the semi-trucks because of all the Buckeye stuff you bring to the game.

You know you're a __REAL__ Buckeye when...

45. You do more planning and spend more money on your tailgate party than your own daughter's wedding.

46. You start your own newspaper just so you can get press credentials to go to the game.

47. Your baby wears only scarlet and gray diapers.

You know you're a __REAL__ Buckeye when...

48. You can't wait for the new fall line of Buckeye fashions.

49. You child's first letters are T-B-D-B-I-T-L instead of A-B-C.

50. If you can't get tickets, you stand outside the stadium and chant at visitors leaving early, "If you can't beat the Bucks, you might as well beat the traffic!"

*You know you're a **REAL** Buckeye when...*

51. Your worst nightmare is having to cheer for one
Buckeye squad over the other at the annual
Spring Scrimmage game.

52. Your child's first words are "Go Bucks!"

You know you're a <u>REAL</u> Buckeye when...

*You know you're a **<u>REAL</u>** Buckeye when...*

53. You have a personalized shopping basket at all the Buckeye specialty stores in town.

54. You have to tear out a section of the ceiling to fit in the goal post you tore down after the big game.

55. You rent *Gone with the Wind* because you heard there was a lot of "Scarlet" in it.

56. You keep a chart of all the seats you've sat in at Ohio Stadium, and your dream is to eventually sit in every seat before you die.

57. You have your own pair of designer Buckeye pom-poms.

You know you're a __REAL__ Buckeye when...

58. Your idea of "Great Performances" is the Ohio State Marching Band's pre-game Skull Session instead of a concert at The Met.

59. Your new house looks like a replica of the Horseshoe instead of the split level your spouse wanted.

60. You dress your children like Ohio State football players and cheerleaders...and your children are in their 30s.

You know you're a __REAL__ Buckeye when...

61. Your idea of the perfect honeymoon suite is one of the dorm rooms inside the Horseshoe.

62. You genuflect every time you hear Woody's name.

63. The police ask you to restrain yourself to ringing your home version of the "victory bell" after the game to only one-half hour instead of ten.

You know you're a __REAL__ Buckeye when...

64. You decide which Super Bowl team to root for based on how many Buckeyes are playing on it.

65. You call into the Coach's radio show and start off every time by saying, "Hi, Coach! I'm your biggest supporter!"

66. If Underwater Basketweaving was a Buckeye sport, you'd buy tickets.

You know you're a REAL Buckeye when...

67. The neighbors keep complaining about the chalk lines on your yard.

68. You would like to research Brutus' family tree,
    but you can't figure out which one it is.

You know you're a <u>REAL</u> Buckeye when...

You know you're a __REAL__ Buckeye when...

69. You believe Spring Practice should begin January 2.

70. You've had to explain to the campus police why the car with Michigan plates parked next to yours has been mysteriously buried in Buckeye nuts...again.

71. The last time the doctor drew blood, it came out scarlet and gray.

72. You've got so many Buckeye flags strapped to your house that when a strong wind blows, the house moves.

73. Your mom asks you to quit dying her
cat and dog scarlet and gray.

You know you're a __REAL__ Buckeye when...

74. You end up in the E.R. because you jumped out of the car when your date told you he was from Michigan.

75. If the Buckeyes lose to Michigan, you wear a black mourning armband for six months.

76. You've had to rent a storage locker for your clothes because there wasn't enough room in the closet for all your Buckeye stuff.

You know you're a <u>REAL</u> Buckeye when...

77. Your neighbors didn't appreciate your use of the snow-making machine in June to recreate the great "Snow-Bowl" game in your backyard.

78. When your boss offered you a big promotion, you turned it down because you'd have to move to Ann Arbor.

79. You changed your last name to Ohio because your wife's first name is Carmen.

You know you're a __REAL__ Buckeye when...

80. You start a petition to make it illegal to wear maize and blue within the state line.

81. You watch the game, review the highlights, and tape every sportscast on every station. Then you put in your tape of the game and watch the whole thing over again.

82. You envy the streaker who runs across the field during the game.

You know you're a __REAL__ Buckeye when...

83. Your boss told you that *Dress Down Day* does not mean taking off your shirt and painting yourself scarlet and gray.

84. You go into a fashion dilemma when you can't decide which lucky Buckeye hat to wear to the game.

You know you're a REAL Buckeye when...

You know you're a __REAL__ Buckeye when...

85. You get into a two-hour debate over who got the better parking place at the game.

86. You've written your first children's Buckeye reading primer. "See Brutus. Run, Brutus, run. There's a break in the defense. Run for the touchdown, Brutus. Run, run, run. Touchdown, Brutus, touchdown!"

87. Every Christmas, you mail bifocals to all the Big Ten referees.

88. You replace the artificial turf in your basement with Ohio State prescription grass and 400 grow lights.

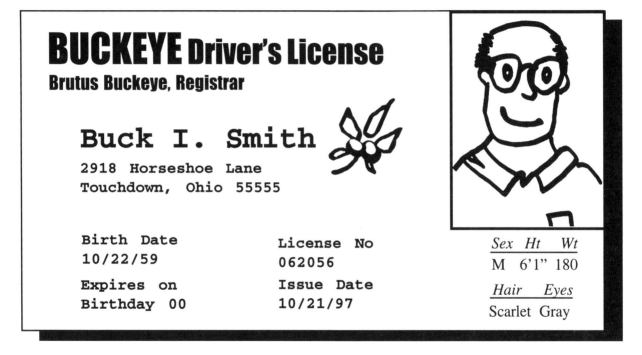

BUCKEYE Driver's License
Brutus Buckeye, Registrar

Buck I. Smith

2918 Horseshoe Lane
Touchdown, Ohio 55555

Birth Date
10/22/59

Expires on
Birthday 00

License No
062056

Issue Date
10/21/97

Sex Ht Wt
M 6'1" 180

Hair   Eyes
Scarlet Gray

89. You legally change your name to Buck I. Smith.

You know you're a __REAL__ Buckeye when...

90. You ship off a package of Buckeye stuff to the Pope at the Vatican in hopes of converting him from a Notre Dame fan to an Ohio State fan.

91. You watch <u>and</u> listen to TV <u>and</u> radio coverage of the Ohio State game simultaneously to compare play-by-play.

92. You tell your kids that they're on their own for college because Daddy needs a new tailgate RV.

You know you're a __REAL__ Buckeye when...

93. Your idea of a romantic evening consists of a cold beer, pretzels, the scouting report on next year's freshmen Buckeyes, and a tape of the 1997 Rose Bowl victory.

94. You brag about __almost__ making the Ohio State Marching Band, but were cut due to bad ankles.

95. You ask the minister to hold up the wedding ceremony until the game is over.

96. After a touchdown, the team gets penalized
because **_you're_** celebrating too much.

97. You'd rather get "A" deck seats in the lottery for Ohio State football tickets than win big money in the state lottery.

You know you're a __REAL__ Buckeye when...

98. You're still using your Ohio State Student ID even though you graduated in 1965.

99. You cheer so loudly for the Buckeyes that when the cheerleaders lose one of their megaphones, they ask you to come down to the field and fill in.

100. The man behind you keeps asking you to quit waving your "Buckeyes are #1" foam finger around during the movie.

101. You've thrown your back out from the
     number of Buckeye necklaces you wear.

Do you know someone
who's a real Buckeye ✤ "nut"?

Please send me ___ copies of "101 Ways to Tell If You're a Real Buckeye!"

Name:_____

Address:_____

City:_____   State:_____   Zip:_____

Telephone: (___)_____   E-mail address:_____

Enclosed is my check (payable to Brus & Sasscer Publishing) or money order—$6.95 for each book, plus $2 for shipping and handling for the first book and $1 for each additional copy.

Ohio residents please add 5.75 percent state sales tax.

Send your order to: Brus & Sasscer Publishing, "Buckeyes," 3000B East Main Street, #354, Columbus, OH 43209.

/